Danger Girls

'Don't come near me, or I'll jump – and take my son with me.' The man who uttered the threat was crouched on a rooftop parapet in London, and his words meant a double tragedy, for he was perched fifteen metres above the street.

Down below, a young Scots policewoman, Margaret Cleland, was being told the grim facts by an inspector. She had been carrying out routine duties when she received an urgent message to help the police who were trying to resolve the desperate situation on the roof . . .

Margaret Cleland is only one of the girls you'll find in this book who suddenly found themselves thrust into appallingly dangerous situations and left to fend for themselves. Taken from places as far away as Canada, America and Australia, as long ago as the fifteenth century and as recently as 1964, here are sixteen exciting true stories of female heroism in the face of overwhelming odds.

Robin May is a journalist and author. He has been fascinated by the American West for many years and has written several books about it, including two Beaver paperbacks, *True Adventures of the Wild West* and *Facts and Feats of the Wild West*. He is also the author of two Beaver quiz books, *Show-Biz Quiz* and *History Quiz*.

DANGER GIRLS!

Robin May

Illustrated by Trevor Parkin

Beaver Books

First published in 1980 by
The Hamlyn Publishing Group Limited
London · New York · Sydney · Toronto
Astronaut House, Feltham, Middlesex, England

© Copyright Text Robin May 1980
© Copyright Illustrations The Hamlyn Publishing
Group Limited
ISBN 0 600 34119 4

Set, printed and bound in Great Britain by
Cox & Wyman Limited, Reading
Set in Monotype Bembo

Contents

Prelude to Danger

Only two, perhaps three, of the girls in this book are well known. Many of them had adventures so desperate that the word 'danger' is perhaps too mild to describe the perils they endured. All of them were in their teens or early twenties and all in their different ways showed great courage.

Courage, of course, is not necessarily linked with the sort of danger described in this book. The 1978 *Woman's Own* Children of Courage awards had examples of both sorts of courage. Eleven-year-old Portia Ritchie who, with her father, was swept downstream in a flooding, swollen river after a boating accident, won an award. They managed to grab a tree root that stuck out from a submerged island and for forty-five seemingly endless minutes Portia comforted her exhausted father, who said he would not have survived without her. He kept on saying: 'I don't think I can last much longer,' said Portia, but she just went on telling him that it would be all right. It was!

Another award winner was twelve-year-old Karen Campbell, born a spastic, who cannot move her legs and can only use her arms a little. She has a spinal disease and has constantly had to have major operations. But, says the warden of her special school, 'she lights up the place by being happy and cheerful and, despite her disabilities, tries to assist in as many ways as possible.' She has never felt sorry for herself. Courage can take many different forms.

And now to our danger girls, beginning with one who saved her father's fort!

1 Defending Castle Dangerous

'Run, Mademoiselle, run! The Indians! Look!'

Madeleine turned in the direction the man was pointing and saw her father's workers and other settlers being cut down by Iroquois braves yelling triumphantly as they ran. She started to race for the fort, the fort that only had two soldiers, the fort that she must try and defend because her father was away. How long could she hold out?

As she ran, she counted her forces in her mind. There was herself, Madeleine de Verchères, a not-very-tall fourteen-year-old. There were her two brothers, aged twelve and ten. There were the two soldiers, an old man of eighty, and some women and children. And there was the man who had warned her of the Indians. It was not much of an army to hold off a war party of Iroquois warriors, the most feared Indians in North America.

The date was 22nd October 1692, and the place, Fort Verchères, on the south bank of the St Lawrence River some thirty kilometres below Montreal in Canada.

No one called the fort by its proper name, but by its nickname, Castle Dangerous. Peace was something that few of the inhabitants of that battle-scarred area knew much about, for long before this, the French who had founded New France (now the province of Quebec) had fallen out with the Iroquois. The French had plenty of Indian allies, but none were as powerful as the mighty Iroquois who lived in what is now northern New York State and lorded it far beyond that area.

What made Castle Dangerous so particularly hazardous was its position, for it was only a short distance from the route the Iroquois took when they were raiding northwards. And the Iroquois that autumn were very angry, for some of their tribe, who had been at peace with the white man, had been treacherously seized and sent to work in French galley ships as slaves – thousands of kilometres from their beloved homeland. These unfortunates found themselves chained to benches, rowing and being lashed in galleys in the Mediterranean. Many white men were to die because of this folly.

Yet things had seemed peaceful enough that autumn at the fort, so much so that Madeleine's father, the Sieur de Verchères, and Madeleine's mother, had felt able to go to the capital, Quebec. As for the fort itself, it seemed strong enough, with a wooden stockade around it and a blockhouse connected to it by a covered passage. There was a landing beside the river and it was there that the alarm had been given, too late to save the people in the fields who had been cutting the corn and picking pumpkins and the last of the melons and fruit from trees that were groaning under their load.

With Iroquois bullets cutting into the dust beside her, Madeleine reached the gate of the fort. 'To arms! To arms!' she called hopefully, expecting at least to see the two soldiers and get some covering fire from them. The cowardly pair had already hidden in the blockhouse.

By the gate were two weeping women whose husbands

had just been killed in the fields. 'Inside at once with you. There is much to be done!' Madeleine urged them, then pushed them through the gate, rushed through herself and shut it behind her, driving the crossbeams firmly into place.

Noting that some palisades had fallen down, she ordered every available woman to help her put them back, then ran to find her two-man army. She went into the block-house and saw the pair, one of them hiding in a corner and the other holding a lighted match.

'What are you doing with that?' she cried.

'I'm going to light the powder and blow us all up,' answered the soldier.

'You are a miserable coward,' said Madeleine. 'Get out of here!' He got out.

Madeleine returned to the fort and assembled her tiny force. 'Let us fight to the death,' she said to her brothers. 'Remember that we are fighting for our father and our religion. Remember that our father has taught you that gentlemen are born to shed their blood for the service of God and the king.'

She then posted the boys and the soldiers at the loopholes, where they began to fire at the Indians. The fort looked strong enough from the outside and the Iroquois were reluctant to make a frontal assault as they did not know the size of the garrison. To keep them guessing she had the men racing from one loophole to the next to give an impression of far more men than she actually had, meanwhile the women loaded the guns for the men and boys.

'We will fire the cannon!' Madeleine now ordered. 'That will impress our foes. And it may be heard by our soldiers who are far from the fort hunting.' 'If they are alive still,' she said to herself. They were not.

Now the women and children began to wilt under the strain and several started screaming.

'Be quiet!' Madeleine ordered. 'If the Iroquois hear you they will learn the truth and attack us!' The noise died away.

Suddenly, a canoe was seen approaching the landing and in it were a settler and his family. The soldiers refused to go to their aid, so Madeleine decided that she must saunter out herself. It might make the Indians feel that a trap had been laid to draw them near the fort where the defenders would launch an assault on them.

Out of the gate went Madeleine as if she had not a care in the world. She reached the landing, welcomed the settlers, and escorted them back – and the Indians did nothing at all!

Now she had an extra man in her little army. She ordered the rate of fire to be stepped up, but a storm broke out and she feared a night attack under its cover. She gathered her six-strong army together and made a speech.

'God has saved us today from the hands of our enemies,' said the dauntless young leader, 'but we must take care not to fall into their snares tonight. I will take charge of the fort with an old man of eighty and another who has never fired a gun, and you, Pierre Fontaine (the newly arrived settler), with La Bonté and Gachet (the soldiers), will go to the blockhouse with the women and children, because that is the strongest place. If I'm taken, don't surrender, even if I'm cut to pieces and burned before your eyes. The enemy cannot hurt you in the blockhouse if you make the least show of a fight.'

Then Madeleine stationed her brothers on two of the fort's bastions, while she and the servant took charge of the other two. So the fort had as sentinels that stormy night a girl, two small boys and a man who did not know how to fire his gun. They shouted 'All's well!' as best they could over the storm until, at around one in the morning, the servant, who was nearest the gate, shouted: 'Mademoiselle, I hear something!'

Madeleine ran to the gate. Through a chink she could see the few cattle that the Indians had not killed barely outlined on the snow-covered ground. Should she risk opening the gate to let them in, or was it a crafty Iroquois trick?

Madeleine was very sure. 'You don't know the Iroquois' tricks as I do,' she said firmly. 'They will be behind the cattle, dressed in the skins of animals, and waiting to get into the fort if we are simple enough to open the gate.'

The others still disagreed and finally Madeleine decided the risk must be taken to get more food. She had her brother posted by the gate if there was any trouble, then she and the servant slipped out and brought the cattle in. It had not been an Iroquois ruse. The red men had been sheltering from the storm and not taken advantage of the cattle.

Yet it had been a near thing. Long after the fight, the Indians confessed that they had planned an attack that night, but had decided not to because the garrison seemed so much on its guard. If they had only known how few defenders there actually were!

When day dawned everyone in the fort seemed more cheerful, especially now that they knew they could not starve. Assuming they could hold out, of course! Somehow they had to, for the Iroquois had cruel ways of making their captives die. Lucky ones were adopted into their tribe; the unlucky perished at the stake. They were expected to die bravely, shouting defiance at their captors, who would admire them greatly for their courage. But only the very valiant could endure such torments and still have the strength to shout back at their tormentors.

Meanwhile Madeleine was having trouble with Pierre Fontaine's wife, who had not long reached Canada from Paris. Madeleine later wrote how timid Madame Fontaine was, 'as all Parisian women are!'

Her husband was made of sterner stuff. 'I will never abandon this fort while Mademoiselle Madeleine is here,' he said firmly, and, indeed, there was nowhere else to go. Except to the stake.

'I will never abandon it,' said Madeleine. 'I would rather die first. If the Indians get possession of any French fort, they will think they can capture others and will be bolder than ever.'

The siege continued for a whole week and there was little respite from alarms and the crack of bullets. But the Iroquois were kept at a distance. They did not dare risk a frontal attack across the open ground around the fort.

As for Madeleine, she barely snatched more than a few minutes sleep during all that seemingly endless week. She never retired to her father's house in the fort, but was always on the bastion or visiting the blockhouse, keeping up the spirits of the defenders and telling them that help must surely come.

And come it did. News had reached the outside world of the attack and forty men commanded by Lieutenant La Mounerie were sent to relieve the garrison.

They came stealthily by night, for they had no way of knowing whether the fort had been taken or not. One of the sentinels heard a sound and cried out: 'Who goes there?' Madeleine, who had been enjoying a few moments' doze with her head slumped on a table, and with her gun cradled in her arms, was awake in an instant. She mounted the bastion.

'Who are you?' she called.

'We are Frenchmen: it is La Mounerie who comes to your help,' called the lieutenant.

Ordering a sentinel to the gate, Madeleine went down to the landing to meet the detachment. Lieutenant La Mounerie gazed in astonishment at the small pale, tired figure in front of him who held herself like a soldier.

'Monsieur, I surrender my arms to you,' said Madeleine, giving the lieutenant a fine military salute.

'Mademoiselle, they are in good hands,' said the gallant young officer.

He accompanied her to the fort, inspected it very thoroughly, and found everything satisfactory, with the sentinels all at their posts.

'It is time they were relieved,' said Madeleine. 'We have not been off our bastions for a week.'

*   *   *   *   *   *

So ended one of the most gallant episodes in the entire history of the wars between Indians and whites in North America. In the story of French Canada Madeleine remains an outstanding personality. Her feat thrilled all New France and France itself, and is vividly remembered by all Canadians to this day.

After it, she was summoned to meet the governor in Quebec and modestly and simply told him the tale of Castle Dangerous and its siege. She married and had a large family, none of whom had to face such hardships and show such heroism, determination and military skill as their wonderful mother had once shown in a time of desperate peril.

2　Parachuted into Peril

'Your life will be in constant danger,' they warned her,
and they gave her a poison pill in case she was captured and
tortured. Then they dropped her into France. Violette
Szabo's new life of danger was under way.

Not that she had any regrets. She was a volunteer who
wanted to avenge her husband's death. Besides, she had
always loved the thought of adventure and now she had
parachute-jumped into the thick of one.

Violette had been born in 1921. She was the daughter of
a British car salesman named Bushell, who had married a
French girl he met during the First World War of 1914–18.
By the time the family moved back to Britain to live in
London in 1932, Violette spoke French like a native.

She became very keen on shooting, which meant visiting
amusement arcades in London's West End. By the age of
fourteen, she was a first-rate shot. She longed for an adven-
turous life, and found the dress shop where she worked
later rather tame, so tame that she ran away to France and
had to be brought back.

Back meant back to more shop work, then in 1939 war
broke out once more and Violette found herself hard at
work in the Women's Land Army, a body of girls and

women drafted into the countryside to replace farmworkers who were now soldiers. It might not be exciting, but it was better than serving in any shop.

She managed to get home to her parents in Brixton from time to time, and one day brought a Free French officer, Étienne Szabo, home to meet them both. Étienne, a member of the legendary French Foreign Legion, was one of many Frenchmen now serving overseas because their beloved homeland had fallen into the clutches of the Germans in 1940.

He and Violette fell in love and were soon married. There was no point in long engagements in those desperate days. Happiness had to be snatched when and where it could be found.

There was precious little of it for the young lovers. Étienne was posted to North Africa and Violette joined the Women's Royal Army Corps as a plane-spotter, a far more exciting job for her than working on the land. However, she had to leave to have a baby daughter, Tania, who was born in 1942. Soon came the tragic news that Étienne had been killed in action. It was soon after she was over the first bitter shock that she made her vow of vengeance.

Not long afterwards she was summoned to an interview with an army officer in a government building in London's Whitehall. She was asked many questions, but the vital one was whether she spoke French like a native or not, and, of course, she did.

'Now Mrs Szabo,' said the keen-eyed officer, 'if you want to you can become a spy with the SOE – that's the Special Operations Executive.' Then he warned her – as if she needed to be told – that the job was very dangerous.

'You may find yourself wrecking buildings – factories and so on', said the officer, 'You may be blowing up bridges or trains. Make no mistake: if you're caught by the Germans, they'll almost certainly shoot you.'

'I don't mind dying the way my husband did,' said Violette.

So began a tough training course on which Violette found herself firing revolvers and machine guns, handling explosives and learning all about them, parachuting, and studying less dramatic but vital things like map reading and Morse-signalling.

By the time she had finished those intensive weeks of training, she was better equipped than most soldiers for coping with emergencies by day or night, and possessed many of the skills of a first-rate criminal! She also had a new name, Corinne Leroy, and was told that 'Corinne' was a secretary from the French port of Le Havre. Naturally, she was given the forged documents to prove it.

Her first mission was to be in Normandy, where she was to be dropped with other agents to locate French Resistance groups and find out just how much they could help when the Allies landed to free France and occupied Europe. For now it was 1944 and only a few weeks away from that epic day, D-Day, 6th June, when British, American, Canadian and Free French forces would invade the beaches of Normandy. Not that Violette and her fellow agents knew the date – just that the great day was coming.

There was one last thing to be attended to. Violette was handed a poison pill. 'In case you're captured and tortured,' she was told, but she was only too well aware of what would happen to her in the hands of the dreaded German secret police, the Gestapo. Gestapo interviewers wanted answers fast and would use any means to get them.

For two weeks after she was dropped Violette picked up plenty of useful information as she travelled through north-

ern France. She got as far as Paris and took a little time off
to buy some dresses for herself and one for her daughter
Tania. A day or two later, she was safely back in Britain.
Her first mission had been successfully accomplished in
perfect safety.

The second one came along fast enough. The very day
after D-Day she was parachuted into France once more, this
time with three men. They landed near a village called
Sussac and Violette's job was to help a Resistance leader
called Anastasie get information and plans of attack to other
fighters.

Anastasie was an important man in the area and Violette
was determined to guard him well. When she clambered
into his Citröen car, she had a Sten gun ready for instant
action in the suitcase beside her on the seat.

Everything seemed to be going smoothly until they were
leaving a small village, when they ran into a German
ambush. Violette saw the soldiers' caps behind the hedge.

'Stop the car!' she shouted, and opened fire with her
Sten as she leapt out. Her companion was close behind her
and a bitter battle commenced. Violette was wounded, and
to make things worse, her ankle, which had been damaged
in training jumps by parachute, suddenly let her down as it
gave way beneath her.

Thinking only of Anastasie, she shouted: 'Run! It's
your only chance to escape.'

Anastasie fired a last burst with his machine gun, then
started off across the meadows. It appalled him to leave the
valiant girl behind, but he had no choice. He flung her a
last glance and saw her out of ammunition and kicking
and scratching the Germans who had caught her.

There is little more to tell. Even torture could not
make her betray her comrades, and finally, after many

months and transfers from one hellish prison to another, she was shot in the dreaded Ravensbruck concentration camp for women in January 1945, not long before the war ended.

A year later little Tania went to Buckingham Palace in the dress that her beautiful, brave mother had bought for her in Paris, and was given Violette's George Cross, the highest award that her country could bestow on her for her bravery, by King George VI. Much later a film was made of her story, *Carve her Name with Pride*, starring Virginia McKenna, so that millions were able to learn the story of Violette, GC.

3   The Horseback Sea Rescue

It was a grand day for riding through the bush, and sixteen-year-old Grace Bussell was enjoying every minute of it. She was the daughter of one of Western Australia's first settlers, and with her that December day in 1876 was one of her father's Aboriginal stockmen, Sam Isaacs.

They rode out of the bush and towards the edge of a cliff overlooking the sea. Suddenly, they froze in horror, for there below them was a steamship in distress and, worse still, a lifeboat had just overturned. They could see people being sucked under the waves.

The cliffs were steep but Grace and her companion did not hesitate. Risking falls and certain death they started the tortuous climb down to the beach.

The ship was a coastal steamer, the *Georgette*, bound for Adelaide. Almost 300 kilometres out of Freemantle, she had sprung a leak and her captain realised at once that he had little chance of saving her. What mattered therefore was the safety of the passengers, forty-eight of them, but, alas, the *Georgette* was short of lifeboats, and they were in poor shape. The only official lifeboat was as leaky as the ship herself and sank in a matter of moments, drowning all its eight occupants.

The captain decided to try and run the vessel ashore before she, too, sank, but the *Georgette* grounded when she was still some way out.

There was one other boat on board, which was rapidly launched, but it had scarcely left the ship's side when it overturned. It took nearly an hour for the crew to right it and get it back alongside. Women and children were lowered down into it, and it set out again for the shore, only to capsize again in two and a half fathoms of raging water. Some of its occupants were drowned straight away, others clung desperately to the sides of the boat.

The captain swept the coastline through his telescope, but it was a wild and desolate stretch and there was no one to be seen. In fact, he was wrong, for Grace and Sam were already descending the cliffs.

They were spotted by passengers and crew as they made their perilous descent, and to everyone's amazement the pair reached the beach safely. Without a moment's hesitation they plunged into the foaming sea.

Grace was a true pioneer, as much at home on a horse as on her two feet, but it seemed impossible to those watching so anxiously that she and Sam could ever reach the overturned boat. However, despite heart-stopping stumbles, they finally succeeded.

'Take my child! Take mine!' the mothers called.

Quickly Grace placed two small children in front of her on the saddle. Grasping hold of a third she started for the shore. Meanwhile, Sam collected his load and followed her.

It was a nightmare ride, but Grace sensibly took her time, and, although on several occasions they were almost swept away, they reached the shore.

Grace put her living load gently down on the beach and

rode straight back into the surf once again. On this journey she returned with children and mothers clinging on to her skirt on each side of her.

This heroic shuttle-service continued for four hours until the valiant girl and her equally brave companion had rescued every surviving passenger. Then Grace collapsed utterly exhausted.

After a few moments, she looked up and realised that many of the survivors were even more exhausted than she was, and that unless food and warm clothing were brought to them, there would be more deaths. So she mounted her horse once more and galloped off north towards her home some fifteen kilometres away at Busselton, named after her family.

When she got there, she fell from her horse and fainted. It was some time before her anxious parents could find out what had happened to get her into this drenched and exhausted state.

When she came to, she managed to gasp out: 'There's been a shipwreck down the coast. Sam and I got as many as we could ashore. They're lying on the beach. Sam's doing his best to look after them, but they need help, father!'

Grace's sister hastily collected some food and blankets and galloped away to the beach, while her father got the family wagon ready and set off to bring all the survivors back home to recover. Grace stayed behind. After her tremendous ordeal, she was in dire need of rest.

The next morning, all the survivors arrived in the wagon and told Grace's parents the full story of her heroism. Nor was Sam's part in the rescue forgotten. The whole party stayed at the house for several days while they regained their strength after their terrible adventure.

Grace Bussell's heroism caused a great stir throughout the British Empire and Commonwealth. It was hardly surprising, for it remains one of the most magnificent epics in the long story of rescues from the sea. She was awarded the much prized medal of the Royal Humane Society, and Sam Isaacs, too, was given a medal for his bravery. The British government gave Grace a special presentation watch.

The rest of her life was more peaceful. She later married a fellow Australian and lived until 1935, almost half a century after her glorious feat.

4 To Save a Prince

The loud knocking woke Flora at once. She dressed quickly, wondering who it could be at this late hour. Perhaps it was soldiers, for these were dangerous times. There were troops everywhere in the Highlands searching for Prince Charles Edward Stuart – Bonnie Prince Charlie – who had tried to win the British throne for his father James. Perhaps the troops had tracked him down to her island of South Uist in the Hebrides.

The Prince and his Highlanders had been defeated by King George II's soldiers on Culloden Moor in April 1746, and it was now late June. Prince Charlie had been on the run since the battle. He had indeed reached Flora's island.

Flora Macdonald was a slim, attractive, twenty-three year old and normally lived with her stepfather on the Isle of Skye, but that June night found her with her brother in South Uist where she had been born. She was alone in the house.

Flora ran to the door. She knew both the men who stood there. One was a lively Irish soldier, Felix O'Neill, the other was a distant relative of her's named Neil Mac-Eachain.

She was not surprised to see them. Though she and her stepfather were loyal to the British king, many of her friends had fought against him at Culloden, including these two men. She realised that they were fleeing from the fierce, red-coated soldiers.

'There's a man outside, Flora,' said one of the men, 'and he needs your help.'

Flora's heart leapt for she knew it must be the Prince. A young man stepped out of the darkness smiling and Flora invited him in and gave the trio some food.

'I wish to go to Skye, Miss Macdonald. Will you be so kind as to help me?'

Flora agreed. It must be stressed that she did so from sheer kindness to a fellow human being, not because she supported him. She did so knowing that it would turn her into a traitor, which makes her story all the more marvellous.

There was plenty of thinking and planning to be done. Flora gave the trio food and they left to await news of just how the escape could be managed.

The soldiers were not far behind the fugitive. Soon they were searching the island, while the Prince kept one step ahead of them, darting from cave to cave. Six days later he heard that he must go to Benbecula, a small island between North and South Uist. Flora would join him there.

Flora's stepfather had reluctantly agreed to help in the escape. Though loyal to King George, he made out a pass for her and had written a letter to her mother in Skye which said that Flora was returning home with her serving girl, 'Betty Burke, an Irish girl'. Betty was to be none other than the Prince.

Meanwhile, a boat had been found to take the Prince to Skye, with six members of the Clan Donald.

The escaping party assembled in a hut on Benbecula and were enjoying a meal, when suddenly there was a knock on the door.

'The soldiers have landed!' a clansman told them. 'They're heading this way!'

The Prince and the rest of them grabbed what they could and raced down to the shore where they were rowed to another part of the island. Then in excellent spirits they finished their meal.

The next evening it was time to set out for Skye. Flora helped the Prince into his costume, which was a printed linen gown with a hooded cloak. The Prince became very annoyed with the hood, cursing it a thousand times, apparently!

'And I want a pistol to wear under my skirts,' he demanded.

'No, sir!' said Flora firmly. 'In case you are searched.'

'Then I'll have this small cudgel instead,' said Prince Charlie, and hid it away.

That night the Prince, with one of his friends and Flora, set out in a small boat with a mast and oars. There were four oarsmen and a helmsman.

The waves and wind were against them and they were driven back to shore. Later they set out again. It was now pitch dark, but they were making good headway when the wind sprang up again. They were helpless without a compass and stopped rowing until dawn broke.

Still fate was against them, for there was a thick mist that morning. They went on drifting, then the tide pulled them towards the Skye shore.

There were soldiers keeping a look-out on the shore, and some of them ran away to report the sighting of the boat. The Prince's party rowed on and found a lonely cove

where they landed and had breakfast. Then Flora walked on to ask another of her clan, Macdonald of Kingsburgh, for help and rest. He agreed to help.

The tall Prince did not make an ideal girl. He tended to take long steps and would lift his skirts to cross a brook. Later, when he was with Macdonald of Kingsburgh, he was seen by people returning from church, who were amazed to see the 'maid' arguing with the most important man in the neighbourhood.

After a night under cover with Macdonald, the weary party split up. The Prince gave Flora a lock of his hair, but they were to meet just once more for a final parting in an inn at Portree.

'For all that has happened,' said the Prince, 'I hope we shall meet in St James's yet!' By that he meant in London, though he must have known that his cause was hopelessly lost by then. Then the Prince and the girl who had saved him parted for ever. The Prince escaped to France, but Flora was soon arrested on suspicion of aiding him and finally found herself imprisoned in the Tower of London.

Yet she found that most Englishmen admired her enormously. They thought she was wonderful and a great heroine, which, of course, she was. Nearly every Englishman and Scot rejoiced when she was pardoned and set free after a year.

She married another Macdonald and had a large family. For a time they lived in America, and when the American colonies rebelled against Britain in 1775, Flora and her husband and their clansmen who had gone with them remained loyal to the Crown. As the world knows, she was on the wrong side!

Flora returned to her beloved Scotland, and when she died in 1790, she was given the grandest funeral the islands had ever known. Pipers played and, in the Highland fashion, there was feasting, drinking and dancing in her honour. She was – and she still is – Scotland's most beloved heroine.

5   Fear in the Forest

Life seemed very good to fourteen-year-old Jemima Boone that July day in 1776. With her friends Betsey and Fanny Callaway, she was canoeing on the river near Boonesborough, the fort founded by her famous father, Daniel Boone, deep in Indian country.

Jemima was trailing her foot in the water, having cut it on a piece of cane stubble. She was staring at the dark forests beyond and thinking of her father's many adventures in this wild area, known as Kentucky's Dark and Bloody Ground.

'Let's go and pick some flowers in the woods,' said Betsey, who was sixteen. Fanny, fourteen like Jemima, enthusiastically agreed.

'Reckon we'd better not,' said Jemima, who had been well trained by her father. 'Pa says that the Shawnees look like going on the warpath, and there ain't no sense goin' for a stroll in the woods this side of the river. The trees look mighty thick over yonder.'

As she spoke, the current caught the canoe and sent it gently towards a gravel bank. Just as they hit it, Indians with painted faces and scalps shaved of hair except for scalplocks, burst out of the cane and grabbed the boat.

Fanny had the paddle and started hitting the nearest Indian, but the wood split. All three girls screamed, but not for long. Hands silenced them and they were dragged through the shallows and into the cover of the trees.

They still dared not scream, with tomahawks and vicious-looking knives raised over them. Then a brave spoke in English.

'White girls keep quiet!' he threatened, and grabbed Betsey's hair to make his point. Moments later they were being rushed away into the menacing forest towards the hills.

Back at the stockaded fort it was a peaceful summer Sunday. Boonesborough lay further west than any other American settlement. It was an arrowhead pointing deep into Indian territory.

This was not the Wild West of Sitting Bull and General Custer and Billy the Kid a century ago, but the even more dangerous first West across the Appalachian Mountains some 500 kilometres from the Atlantic Ocean.

The woods and forests and glades were the domain of Indians who had no reason to love the white men with their hunger for land. Many of the Indians had been driven from homes further east. Now, in 1776, a war was raging between the American colonists and the British, the Colonists resenting being governed by a parliament in London where they were not represented. They had other grudges, too, which were serious enough to have caused a war.

The small fort called Boonesborough housed some 200 men, women and children. Boone and his friends wanted no part in the war back east. Americans themselves were divided about the war, many staying loyal to the Crown, but out in the wilds the war seemed far away. Boone and his companions were hardy pioneer folk, true Westerners, as their children and grandchildren would be after them. They were people who wanted to see what lay beyond the next mountain, to settle where no white man had settled before them, to hunt and trap and be free in a way no Easterner could be.

Daniel Boone was now in his early forties and was already a living legend. He knew this first West as no other white man did. He had fought Indians, befriended them, and was greatly admired and feared by them.

He knew Boonesborough was in danger, though things seemed peaceful enough. The Indians resented the fort on their land, besides which many were already siding with the British. That way they felt there was more chance of saving their land. Whatever happened, Boonesborough would be in the front line of any action. Little did the fort's inhabitants know that terrifying action had already taken place.

The girls had been captured by five Indians and now discovered that two of them were Cherokees and three were Shawnees. The Indians had been on their way to examine the defences of Boonesborough and the leader of the five was a Cherokee, Chief Hanging Maw. Second in importance was the Shawnee son of Chief Black Fish. They had fallen into important hands.

Fortunately, neither tribe was a molester of captive women, but as kilometre after kilometre was covered, the girls' despair grew. A lifetime of misery as the wife of an Indian seemed to stretch before each of them.

Jemima was the first to pull herself together, as befitted the daughter of the great Daniel. She hurled herself on the ground.

'Kill me if you want!' she announced. 'I cannot go further in bare feet.' She then lifted her foot up to show the braves the injury she had received from the cane, which was now far worse.

'White girl no worry,' said Hanging Maw. 'I give you moccasins.' Then he cut the girls' long dresses to their knees. 'We walk faster that way. Wrap legs with what I have cut. You no get scratched that way. Hurry!'

Jemima suddenly recognised the chief, who had once visited her father when they had lived elsewhere. Busily but casually marking the ground under her heel to leave traces for her father, whom she knew would come after them, she told Hanging Maw that she had met him.

'You Daniel Boone's girl?' asked the startled chief.

'That I am,' agreed Jemima.

'What about these girls?'

'They are my sisters,' lied Jemima very sensibly. 'Reckon you ought to let us go. You know what a great warrior my pa is!'

'You make joke,' said Hanging Maw, but Jemima could see he was anxious. The Indians had as high an opinion of Daniel Boone as the whites.

Not that his anxiety helped the girls. All it meant was that they headed into the wilds faster than before. They took a route so bare that traces of their movement would be much harder to spot. From time to time the party split in two. Brooks and creeks were crossed and crossed again, though the general direction remained the same – towards the Ohio River and the Indian villages there.

Not that Jemima and her friends lacked frontier cunning. From babyhood they had been trained for emergencies. Jemima kept falling down in apparent pain, Betsey's high-heeled shoes were ideal for leaving traces, and all of them worked at tearing small shreds off their dresses and dropping them along the trail. They broke small twigs when they could, too. Frontiersmen like Boone and his friends could detect almost invisible signs as well as any Indian.

Betsey's high-heeled shoes did not last long, however, for Hanging Maw soon spotted what she was up to and used his tomahawk to knock the heels off, a grim reminder of what bad behaviour might bring down on her head.

They endured a cold night, for the Indians were not prepared to light a fire. Each girl was made to sit down and tied to a tree while the Indians slept, taking it in turn to watch. Hardly surprisingly, none of the girls slept at all.

The next day they reached a spot where the Indians had tied a pony. Jemima was ordered to ride it because of her foot.

'I cannot ride at all,' she lied, and proved it by falling off at every available opportunity. She would tickle its flank, the pony would rear, and off she would tumble. It was a bruising business, for all that she knew how to fall, but worth every ache and pain for the delays that it caused.

Finally, the Indians became enraged by her clumsiness and one of them gave her a riding lesson – with an unexpected result. The pony was now so furious with all humans that it bit the Indian as he attempted to mount. The Indians got so exasperated that they let the pony loose.

Very reasonably, Hanging Maw now threatened to kill the girls if they continued their delaying tactics, raising his tomahawk to give emphasis to the threat. Much of the time now they found themselved being dragged along the trail by their wrists.

That night they were tied up again and for the second night running forced themselves to eat dried buffalo tongue. Their captors were more cheerful now as they neared their homes and got further and further away from possible pursuers. They became so confident that when they saw a buffalo the next day, they killed it and stopped to have a barbecue. They were over sixty kilometres from where the girls had been captured and only a day's journey away from the Ohio and virtual safety.

The girls were naturally utterly downcast. There was no knowing if rescuers were near. Even Daniel Boone might find their trail impossible to follow. Betsey, the oldest, tried to comfort her two weeping friends, but her own spirits were as low as they could be. Too many white girls had vanished for ever into the wilds since the first English colonists arrived early in the seventeenth century. Were they doomed to be three more?

*   *   *   *   *   *

The girls' absence had soon been discovered on the fatal Sunday.

Betsey and Fanny had a cousin called Flanders, who was in love with Jemima and hoped to marry her. He knew about the canoe expedition and went down to the river bank to be there when the three returned. At once, he saw the empty boat grounded on the far side and after he had called them a few times, he began to get alarmed. The girls, especially his beloved Jemima, were far too sensible to take unnecessary risks. Something had happened!

As soon as he had reached the fort again, he raised the alarm.

The peaceful Sunday calm vanished. Sam Henderson, Betsey's fiancée, was shaving when he heard the shouts. He left his face half shaved, grabbed his rifle and headed for the river bank, followed by dozens more. They stared across the river, standing about in their Sunday best, and helpless without a boat.

Daniel Boone was asleep and had to be woken by his wife Rebecca. He rushed down to the river and tried to calm everyone. Choosing a youth called David Gass to swim the river and bring the canoe back, he ordered the rest of the men to cover the boy as he swam across in case Indians should erupt from the trees. Meanwhile, Richard Callaway, whose two children were with Jemima, and who was ten years older than Daniel Boone, led mounted men to a ford some two kilometres downstream, having arranged to meet Daniel on the far side. Daniel canoed across with five others.

There were plenty of signs to indicate which way the Indians had taken the girls, but night was approaching. The sensible Boone pointed out a few facts to them.

'No good rushing things,' he said. 'You've got to steal up on the Injuns, otherwise the girls'll be tomahawked before you get to them. Ten horses charging at them will give them too much warning. Now why don't you and the boys, Richard, ride north and cut the Injuns' retreat off at the Lower Blue Licks. That's where they'll have to cross the Licking River.'

Callaway reluctantly agreed on caution and rode away with his men. Meanwhile, Boone led his party into the woods.

When they camped for the night, someone said to him: 'Daniel, ain't you forgetting something?'

'What's that?' asked Boone.

'Your moccasins,' was the reply. Boone always wore the sensible shoes the Indians wore.

'So I did!' said Boone, whose fears for Jemima had made him forget them. 'Now I think of it, we ain't equipped proper for this expedition, specially as there'll be a fight at the end of it.

'We're in the wrong clothes, we've no food, and we're powerful short of ammunition.'

He sent David Gass back to the fort to get what was needed, and the boy brought back clothes, food, powder and shot, also the missing moccasins, and as soon as it was light they started up the trail.

At first there was plenty to guide them, thanks to the brave girls, but where the Indians had split up to confuse any pursuers, they wasted a lot of time finding the true direction. Finally, Boone, convinced he knew where the Indians were taking the girls, decided to head straight for the area and not waste time trying to track them.

After he had also convinced his worried companions, who did not like the idea of not following the trail, they started north. They several times crossed the Indians' route, spotting signs that the girls had left. The chase was swift and tough, but they were all frontiersmen, ready for any emergency and always in trim because their lives depended on it.

On the Tuesday morning they reached a ford over the Licking River and there on the far side were fresh moccasin tracks.

'We'll follow the trail now,' said Boone. 'Won't be long till you boys'll see some fightin'!'

They passed the dead buffalo and then, not long before noon, they picked up the scent of smoke and saw tracks on the far side of a creek.

'Here's your orders,' Boone whispered. 'We'll split into two groups and close in real quiet. No one fires till I do — that's an order. And when we do fire, we charge straight into the camp. If we don't, why there'll be three dead girls lying there for us to bury!'

They closed in on the Indian camp. Boone could see

Betsey sitting with her back against a tree, and beside her were Jemima and Fanny resting their weary heads in her lap.

Boone noted the positions of the Indians. One was getting ready to cook buffalo, another was lighting a pipe – Boone noted that he was the sentry – a third was gathering sticks for a fire. Then he saw the other two, realising with amazement that one of them was Hanging Maw.

Suddenly, one of the rescuers impatiently fired his gun. Hardly pausing to be annoyed, Boone raised his rifle and fired. The Indians were already heading to kill their prisoners, but the white men's aim was good.

'That's daddy!' shouted Jemima joyously. An Indian hurled his tomahawk at Betsey's head; she moved and it thudded into a tree. But she was in worse peril from a white man who thought she was an Indian: certainly after her terrible ordeal, and with her dress shortened and her skin browned by exposure and dirt, she did not look like a white girl, and the charging man was just about to dash her brains out with his rifle when Boone seized his arm and urgently said: 'For God's sake don't kill her now. We've come all this way to save her!'

At least two of the Indians had been badly injured, but Boone did not pursue them. All that mattered was getting the girls, who were all weeping with joy and with shock, back to the fort. Anyway, reasoned Boone, Callaway and his men would run into them.

He was wrong there. The larger party found the fugitives' tracks but let them go. It was lucky that Boone was made of sterner stuff than them, or Calloway would have lost both his daughters.

Great were the rejoicings back in Boonesborough when the girls and their rescuers returned. Betsey was soon

married to her sweetheart, Sam Henderson, who had been with Boone's party. However, Flanders Calloway and John Holder, Fanny's admirer, were told that they would have to wait until the girls were fifteen before the weddings took place.

Jemima lived a long and happy life, and was with her father when he died in 1820 at the grand old age of eighty-five. By then, though he had had more than his share of disappointments, he was famous not just in America but in many other countries, and to this day he is remembered as the first great Westerner. Jemima's pride in him was boundless, and so was his in her. She was a true daughter of a magnificent man.

6 The Saviour of France

'Take her home and give her a good hiding,' the great man told the girl's uncle, and it is hard to blame him. Robert de Baudricourt, commandant of the castle of Vaucouleurs, was a busy man.

His peace had been disturbed by a peasant girl who claimed to have heard the voices of saints and angels, demanded to see the Dauphin, the as yet uncrowned King of France, and was prepared to drive the English out of France! The times were far too bad to have hysterical girls thrusting themselves forward in a most troublesome way and suggesting that they could save the nation.

Which, of course, is just what Joan of Arc, the most beloved heroine of France, and the admiration of everyone who has ever read her story, did. Her life is one of the miracles of history, so much so that some snobbish people have claimed that she must have been a nobleman's daughter, despite a total lack of evidence to suggest that she was anything of the kind.

Though naturally many legends accumulated about her in her own lifetime, the hard facts of her career are well-documented. She was born around 1412 in Lorraine at the little village of Domrémy, her father being a prosperous farmer there. She seems to have been quite good-looking, on the dark side, strongly built and with a voice that was low but commanded attention.

She was very religious, naturally, even scolding the churchwarden when he forgot to ring the bell. She first heard her famous 'voices' when she was thirteen and they never ceased to guide her. Those who think they were figments of her imagination – she was always shy about them – have to face the facts that the saints – Michael, Catherine and Margaret – were very practical and very demanding.

They told her to go to the castle of Vaucouleurs where Robert de Baudricourt would send her to the Dauphin. She would be given the task of beating the hated English and would then lead the Dauphin to his coronation in the city of Rheims.

At this time England officially ruled France because of King Henry V's great victory at Agincourt in 1415 and subsequent marriage to a French princess. His young son was now Henry VI, the ruler of both countries. With the mighty Dukedom of Burgundy (now part of France) backing the English, it was all the wretched Dauphin and his followers could do to survive.

The first trip to Vaucouleurs was not a success, as we have seen, but support for Joan was growing, not least because of a prophecy that a maid from Lorraine would save France. And things were getting worse. The war swept over the area round Domrémy and the villagers had to flee for their lives. The great city of Orléans was being besieged by the English and if it fell, what hope could there be for the Dauphin's cause?

With her voices urging action, Joan returned to Vaucouleurs and was soon convincing people that she must be given help to reach the Dauphin. The turning point came when the Duke of Lorraine himself was won over. He gave her a safe-conduct, which meant that Robert de Baudricourt, too, had to climb down and help her. Having had her examined by a priest to see if the Devil had her in his clutches, he gave her a sword and ordered an escort of eight men to accompany her on her dangerous journey. She wore a man's clothes.

They headed for Chinon, where the Dauphin was cowering, and the men, some of whom had been quite prepared to harm her, were all won over to her cause. Eleven days after setting out they reached their goal.

The story goes that Joan detected the Dauphin in a vast crowd of courtiers, so proving to his satisfaction—for he had disguised himself – that she recognised the blood royal. True or not, he could hardly help being interested in someone whose mission it was to have him crowned king of France. First, however, he sent her to be examined by priests and other experts. They were a little surprised that she could neither read nor write – 'Me, I know neither A nor B' she told them – but they approved of her. The Dauphin decided to give her a try. After all, she could hardly make things worse!

Now it was time for action. She was given a fine suit of armour, a banner and a black charger, but so far her only weapon was a small battle-axe. She needed a sword and she knew where it was: buried near an altar in a church. Her voices had told her so. No one knew of this sword, but there it was, a little rusty perhaps, but that was soon remedied. With a band of men, including two of her brothers who had come to join her, she headed for Orléans and immortal fame.

Some have claimed that Joan at once proved herself a

military genius, which, of course, would have been impossible. There were skilled French commanders in the field, especially Dunois, who was in charge of the besieged city. What Joan provided was inspiration, and the miracle was that she turned out to be a first rate soldier and not just a sort of mascot. True, she was impatient. Was not God on her side? But she was also a born leader, courageous, equally at home with a sword and a lance, and was soon a master of tactics, especially in the use of artillery. Above all she could inspire her men. She even got them to stop swearing!

On 29th April 1429 she entered Orléans with a picked force and at once electrified the defenders. Who would not be inspired by a commander who led attacks on the English bastions at the head of her men? On one occasion she woke at midnight and put on her armour with such speed that she was mounted before her squire was even dressed. He had to pass her her lance through a window as she galloped away to storm an enemy bastion.

Yet before attacking the English she would go round their strong-points urging them to go home, and was most upset when they used most unchristian oaths by way of reply!

When she took the largest bastion, she was wounded in the chest and was carried from the field weeping, but she had triumphed. The English raised the siege and great were the rejoicings. The bells rang out. People shouted: 'It is all over! We are all saved!' As for Joan, she prayed as she stood proudly in her chain mail, and as her commanders looked at her wonderingly.

Now she urged the Dauphin to fight until he possessed Rheims and could be crowned king. The Dauphin left the fighting to others, but the result was the same. The French went on winning and the English and their allies

c

began to feel that they were being defeated by a demon. A Burgundian called her 'a creature in the form of a woman: Heaven knows what it is', while the Duke of Bedford, the English commander said she was a 'minion of the Evil One, called the Maid.'

Even the French leaders were getting rather irritated with her, for they considered her vain and too quick to claim credit for herself. Actually, she only claimed it for God.

Rheims was entered on 16th July and a day later the Dauphin became King Charles VII. Now he must take Paris. Joan knew it and his generals knew it, but Charles wanted a quiet life and Joan was stopping him having one. She went on fighting until she found that Charles the Victorious, as he styled himself, had ordered his army to cease fighting. Poor Joan, trying to capture the capital, had been wounded in the thigh.

She was kept idly at court, while the English king Henry VI came to France for his coronation, and the Duke of Burgundy, whom Charles imagined had laid aside the sword, began making war on the French again.

The Duke besieged Compiègne, and Joan, who along with her family had been ennobled by Charles – honours she did not want – sped secretly to help the town. Her luck had run out. She led her troops too far from their base and the enemy surrounded her. A Burgundian pulled her from her horse by the lapels of her cloth-of-gold cloak and she fell to the ground.

The wretched king made no effort to help her, though her captors were quite willing to sell her back. 'I advise you to spare no money or effort to recover her,' wrote a bishop, who warned the king that he would otherwise incur the stigma of 'the most disgraceful ingratitude'. The miserable wearer of the Crown took no notice. Joan had served her purpose. She was expendable.

Joan had only one fear. She dreaded falling into the hands of the English. 'We shall burn you, you witch!' they had shouted at her in battle. She tried to escape by jumping from a high tower, but only succeeded in injuring herself.

The English got her, however. They bought her from their Burgundian allies and took her to Rouen where they tried her in front of a French Bishop, Pierre Cauchon, who was in their pocket. His job was to prove her to be a heretic, and a witch as well for good measure, and her trial was rigged so that she had no chance. 'Why have I to be here?' she said at the start of the trial. 'Send me back to God, for that is where I came from!' Her judges had every intention of doing so.

Yet the simple country girl kept the proceedings going for five full months, so shrewd was she with the answers, so dauntless was her spirit.

Solitary confinement in chains, plus insults from her guards in between times, and with no recourse to the Church, finally weakened even Joan's spirit. It seems that she signed a confession of heresy while she was dazed and thinking that all she had to do was start wearing female clothing again.

But when she found that instead of being burnt she was to be imprisoned for life by the English, she dressed as a man again and repudiated her confession. The gleeful English and their French allies knew that they had her at last, for a relapsed heretic was forced to endure the horror of the stake. She had had a fair trial, in theory at least. In fact, it was a disgrace.

She was rushed to the market place in Rouen on 30th May 1431, with 800 men guarding her, so fearful did she appear, even so near death, to her enemies. An Englishman whose name is unknown gave her a simple wooden cross that he had made and she was then burned to death. The flames could not subdue her valiant spirit, for she called 'Jesus' six times as they rose – and as every Frenchman and even some Englishmen wept for her.

Every vestige of her body was destroyed and her ashes were thrown into the River Seine, but she had won. Not only had she halted the English in France and begun the battle to drive them out altogether, but she had inspired Frenchmen of all classes with pure patriotism of a sort that had hardly existed in the Middle Ages before her. And in her family's lifetime her condemnation was reversed by the Church, which finally, in 1920, made her a saint. For centuries before that she had been the very symbol of French national pride, and so she remains to this day.

Condemned to death! That was the verdict, and the method was to be hanging. As sketches and plans of military fortifications had been found in the boot of the suspect, that verdict was hardly surprising – except for the fact that this particular spy was a beautiful girl.

Her name was Pauline Cushman and her lurid life started in the lusty city of New Orleans in Louisiana in the USA in the 1830s. When she was ten years old, her father, who was a trader, moved the family to Grand Rapids, Michigan, more than 1500 kilometres north. Instead of going to school, young Pauline grew up with the local Indians, the Chippewas, who were her father's customers. They called her Laughing Breeze and taught her to ride bareback. She soon learned to shoot like a man and cope with even the fiercest rapids in a canoe. No wonder all the men, Indian and white alike, adored her.

At the age of eighteen, she surprised everyone by deciding to become an actress. She turned out to be a good one, playing in New York in a number of strong dramas, though, or course, her stunning looks may have helped conquer critics and audiences. Whatever the reason, she was soon a real star.

Then in 1861, the American Civil War broke out. The Southern, or Confederate, states broke away from the Union because they wanted to run their own affairs, which included slavery – even though only some Southerners actually had slaves.

Pauline, a Union supporter, went on with her job, until she found herself acting in Kentucky, which was a state in the midst of the fighting and deeply divided between Northern and Southern sympathisers. At that time – 1863 – the state was controlled by Southerners.

They came to see her act. They went further and demanded that she drank a toast to the South. It was no moment for heroics, so she did so. Then she managed to get through the Southern lines to the local Union commander and passed on some useful information to him.

'How would you like to spy for your country, young woman?' asked the commander, and almost before she knew what she was doing. Pauline was swearing an oath of allegiance to the United States and agreeing to go behind the Southern lines and find out all she could about the enemy's troop movements.

The plan was to 'expel' her to the South, having first denounced her as a Southern sympathiser as often and as loudly as possible.

'But see here, Miss Cushman,' said the general who saw her on her way, 'if you get yourself caught by those rebels, there's not a thing we can do for you I fear. Don't go carrying any plans on you, or they'll string you up for sure, even though you are a pretty young gal. This is war!'

So Pauline Cushman became a spy. She acted her new part well and sent back plenty of useful information, some of it smuggled in loaves of bread. Confederate officers used to escort what they thought was a beautiful Southern belle to see the sights – and the fortifications.

One day her luck ran out, and she made things worse by disobeying orders. She drew sketches of the defences of a town called Shelbyville and hid them in a riding boot. On her way back to the Union forces she was stopped by a Southern scouting party, who immediately took her to their headquarters.

The Southern general, though courteous to a lady, was suspicious.

'Why, I do declare, general,' said Pauline hopefully, 'I thought you'd recall that I'm a true Southern gal!'

'Mighty sorry, mam,' said the general, 'but you were headin' for the enemy's lines. I'm forced to send you to be questioned at our base camp.'

On the way to the camp a big storm suddenly blew up and Pauline managed to escape. She was soon recaptured and the escape naturally told against her. Then the plans were found and she was doomed.

The court-martial was short and sharp. She was found guilty and placed in a cell to await her execution by hanging. Then her luck changed once more.

On 25th June 1863, Union troops launched a series of attacks in the Shelbyville area. Pauline listened to the guns drawing nearer and nearer, and, finally, the Southerners fled, leaving her to be rescued by jubilant Union supporters. Then she collapsed and was rushed to the home of a doctor.

While she recovered from her nervous exhaustion, she received a message of congratulations from the President of the United States himself, the great Abraham Lincoln. Another, and rather odd but gratifying reward was an

honorary major's commission in the United States Cavalry.

Naturally, she was now far too well known to be a spy again, so she returned to the stage with a show based on her adventures. She wore her major's uniform. The play was a particular success in the Wild West, where the audience tended to let off six-shooters at the theatre ceiling in her honour.

She liked the free and easy atmosphere of the West so much that she settled there and became a well-known referee in gunfights. If a crowd got too rowdy watching a fight, she would draw her own six-shooter and urge people to step back – or else. They stepped back.

Alas, Pauline had an unhappy marriage and she finally died penniless in San Francisco in 1893. Suddenly, all America remembered that she had been a heroine. She was given a grand military funeral and was buried with veterans of the Civil War. Most of her spying had taken place in the Cumberland Mountains area of the state of Tennessee, so they simply put on her grave marker: *Pauline Cushman, Federal Spy and Scout of the Cumberland.* It can be seen to this day.

8   The Jaws of Death

'Your husband is dead, madame. We have heard how it happened. He died from the terrible cold and from his wounds and his body was thrown from the wagon into the snow. You must have been unconscious from the cold when he died.'

For once Aimée's iron control snapped. Clasping her little son to her, she burst into tears. It was the worst of all the terrible moments she had experienced on the nightmare retreat from Moscow.

Moscow! It seemed an age since she had been reunited there with her husband when Napoleon's Grand Army marched into the deserted city on 14th September 1812. The French Emperor did not only have Frenchmen in his Grand Army. Among his toughest troops were Poles, whose country had been enslaved by Russia and who had joined the great Napoleon believing that Poland would gain its freedom if France defeated Russia.

The French had fought their way across Russia, losing most of their 500,000 men. Aimée's husband, Captain Ladoinski of the Polish Lancers, had been wounded, but not too seriously, and he had been counting the days till he reached Moscow, where his French-born wife was waiting for him with their son. She had been caught in the Russian capital when war had broken out.

Aimée was no great fan of Napoleon, for she feared that he, like the Russians, might betray Poland, but none of that mattered in the joy of reunion. She and her little boy had been watching the troops march into the empty city, all the Russians having fled. They had stared down from their window, but could not spot him, then, suddenly, he was at the door.

That very night Russian saboteurs started a number of fires in the city. Better that their beloved capital should burn than be part of the French Empire!

Despite the fact that many saboteurs were caught and shot, the fires grew worse and worse. They continued for days and only a downpour saved the fifth of the city still standing. Napoleon remained in the capital until 18th October, for he hoped that the Russians would sue for peace. They would not, so he decided to retreat westwards and find winter quarters for his army. He knew he must not be trapped in the snows, but neither he nor his men had any idea just how terrible General Winter, the Russians' best commander, could be . . .

Away from the shell that was Moscow marched Napoleon and 100,000 men, many of them laden with loot they had pillaged. They would have done better to carry food.

With the troops went the Ladoinskis, the handsome captain at the head of his men and Aimée and her son in a baggage wagon.

From the start ferocious Cossack horsemen swept down on the marching army, harassing, killing, then vanishing into the endless forests; on 6th November the first snow began to fall.

Captain Ladoinski was wounded in a fierce action against

the Cossacks and laid beside his wife in the baggage wagon. Day after day she tenderly nursed him.

As if the snows were not enough, such roads as there were had become blocked in many places with abandoned guns, dead horses and broken-down wagons. There were long delays, which all helped the avenging Cossacks, determined to drive the hated invaders from their land.

To add to the horrors, some of the wagon-drivers staged breakdowns, murdering the wounded, throwing the bodies into the snow, and grabbing any loot they could find.

One night the cold was so intense that Aimée might well have died in her sleep if the wagon had not reached the town of Smolensk. Fortunately, a young officer spotted her.

'Quick!' he called to his friends. 'There's a lady here who needs reviving. Brandy someone!'

Soon Aimée was stirring back to life, only to overhear a terrible conversation. At first she thought it was a nightmare.

'Where is Ladoinski?' asked someone.

'Probably died of wounds,' replied another voice.

'It's my belief,' said a third, 'that he's been murdered by those devilish wagon-drivers. Though even they couldn't bring themselves to kill a woman and child.'

She was awake fully now and screamed: 'My husband! Where is he?'

They told her that she and her son had been the only people in the wagon when it reached Smolensk, and tried to comfort her by telling her that her husband was probably in another wagon just behind. Neither she nor they believed it for a moment.

Captain Ladoinski had been much admired in the army, and Prince Eugene Beauharnais, a senior commander, came to Aimée's aid. Wagon-drivers swore that the captain had died and had been thrown out of the wagon. The Prince put Aimée and her son in another wagon and told the driver that if she did not reach Poland safely he would be executed. On the other hand, if she did, he would be properly rewarded.

The nightmare journey continued. Thousands of men of the once proud Grand Army perished from the cold or the Cossacks. It was now nothing more than a ghost army. The suffering of the women and children was indescribable.

Then, near the River Berezina and the Polish border, reinforcements under Marshal Victor arrived, and suddenly, as Aimée lay clasping her son to her, she heard what sounded like her husband's voice calling in Polish: 'Forward, Lancers!'

She leapt up, but could not see him, yet her little boy had heard the voice, too. And yet – could her husband still be alive? He could not of course, for she remembered that the Polish Lancers had left Smolensk before she and her boy had arrived there. It was madness to believe that her wounded husband could be with Victor's army. And yet . . .

Bridges were hastily built over the Berezina, and Prince Eugene rode up to Aimée to tell her that she would soon be in her husband's homeland. Then he turned to the driver of her wagon and reminded him of his duty.

It seemed that the Russians had gone and half the troops had safely crossed the river, when suddenly pandemonium broke out. The Russians had returned.

At once, Aimée's driver took to his heels. What could Aimée do? The two bridges across the river were usable but jammed with men, women and children in every stage of panic. To try and cross meant being crushed to death.

And now Russian bullets were cutting into the desperate throng. Those on the bridge were being killed, crushed or thrown into the icy water. And to add to the horror of the hellish scene, a great thunderstorm began.

With musket balls falling all around her, Aimée laid her son on the ground and then covered him with her body.

Suddenly she saw her husband leading a company of Lancers straight at the Russians! She called to him, but her voice was totally drowned by the din. But he was alive!

By now fear had turned the crowds on the bridges into demons – and all at once the larger one collapsed, drowning everyone on it.

It was at this moment that Aimée thought she was going mad, and she prayed for a swift death for herself and her child. It seemed impossible that her beloved husband could live through this hideous, horrifying scene.

Even now the nightmare was not over. At dawn, as she approached the remaining bridge, it burst into flames, set alight by the retreating French.

In her despair, she tied her child to her and struggled towards the river. All around her Cossacks were plundering the abandoned wagons.

Then a Russian seized her and her screams brought the remnants of the Poles, who were about to cross the river, to her aid. Their officer picked her and the boy up as the Russian fled, and swept them into his saddle.

The Polish officer was . . . Aimée's husband!

Into the swift, icy river they plunged, with musket balls lashing the water beside them. Until Aimeé's shawl fell from her face, Captain Ladoinski had no idea who it was he had saved.

Somehow his sturdy horse got them across the river, and Aimée, who had fainted, awoke in her husband's arms.

He told her how he had been thrown out of the wagon, but had been saved by Polish troops who had found him lying in the snow. He had been told that Aimée was dead!

Prince Eugene was one of the first to be told the good news and came at once to congratulate the happy family. The story of the Ladoinskis raised a flicker of joy throughout the remnants of the army.

Nearly the whole army perished on that terrible retreat, which marked the beginning of the end for Napoleon, an end that was to come on the battlefield of Waterloo in 1815. It was a happier story for the Ladoinskis, for they survived to spend the rest of their lives in well-earned peace.

9 Battle Honour

Her story is like a flash of lightning in a storm. We know little of her after her day – her moment – of glory and nothing of her life before it. Yet her people, the fighting Cheyennes, one of the most famous of all the Indian tribes of the West, named a battle after her. The whites call it the Battle of the Rosebud.

Her name, translated into English, was Buffalo Calf Road Woman and she was the brother of Chief Comes in Sight. Her people had tried vainly to stay on friendly terms with the whites, but their efforts had failed. Now they were allied with the mighty Sioux nation and a few Arapahoes, and white forces were marching on them at their great camp in southern Montana.

The most famous event of those stirring days was the Battle of the Little Big Horn – Custer's Last Stand – on 25th July 1876, where the glory-hunting general and his men were wiped out. We know that Buffalo Calf Road Woman rode with the warriors in that hour-long fight, though we know nothing of what she did. We can guess though, for the warrior girl – and there were few like her – had earned her place with the men a short time before.

True, Indian girls sometimes snatched rifles up when

their camps were attacked, but they were not warriors, like their men. Buffalo Calf Road Woman was such a one and remained one until she died tragically young, of disease in 1879.

On 16th June, nine days before Custer's legendary luck ran out, a force under another Indian-fighter, General George Crook, had appeared near the great Indian camp that had assembled to meet the threat. News of the soldiers was rushed back to the Cheyenne part of the camp by the hunting party that had first seen them. The Sioux, too, were alerted. The chiefs decided to attack with 1000 or so warriors, but, luckily for the whites, there were held up for a vital twenty minutes or so by Indian scouts serving with the soldiers. Then the battle began.

It was a battle of tactics with the Sioux leader Crazy Horse calling the tune. The Indians made lightning attacks on the whites, then appeared to retreat. Some soldiers would pursue them and the results would be fatal.

But the white fire power was greater than anything the Indians could achieve and there were plenty of tense moments. The tensest for the Cheyennes came in the middle of the six-hour action. Chief Comes in Sight led a charge into an enemy flank, a desperate, daring charge that the Indians so loved. Suddenly, a bullet hit his horse and it somersaulted.

Chief Comes in Sight somehow managed to land on his feet and started to zigzag to and fro, shouting defiantly at his enemies. Moments before, he and other chiefs had been daring the enemy to shoot at them, but now he was stranded on his own and facing almost certain death.

Buffalo Calf Road Woman had been busy helping with the horse herds when she saw the somersault that unhorsed her brother. At once she leapt on a horse and raced to his

aid, moving out at full gallop from the trees and the rocks on the north side of the battlefield.

Horse and rider sped past the chief, wheeled round, and pulled up beside him.

Chief Comes in Sight jumped up behind his sister and, with bullets whistling through the air on each side of them, they sped to safety.

The whites were beaten, though General Crook would never admit that he and his men had been defeated at the Rosebud fight. As for the Cheyennes, they gave the action another name and proudly recall it to this day as 'Where the Girl Saved Her Brother'.

10   Rooftop Rescue

'Don't come near me, or I'll jump – and take my son with me!'

The man who uttered the threat was crouched on a rooftop parapet in London, and his words meant a double tragedy, for he was perched fifteen metres above the street.

Down below, a young Scots policewoman, Margaret Cleland, was being told the grim facts by an inspector. She had been carrying out routine duties when she received an urgent message to help the police who were trying to resolve the desperate situation on the roof. At such a moment training counts, training, a cool head and bravery. But no training can give a man or a woman the experience that a situation like this one demands.

She listened as the inspector said: 'He won't speak to us, but he might just talk to you. It's a lot to ask, I know, but will you go up there and get close enough to try and get him talking?'

'I'll do my best,' said Margaret, staring up at the figure outlined against the March sky.

It was a bitter day, cold and windy, enough to make anyone shiver who was just about his ordinary business.

There was nothing ordinary about Margaret's business that day in 1964.

She climbed to the very top of the house and came out on to the roof. Below her, a long long way down, stood a crowd of onlookers staring upwards. She decided that she would not look down again!

Gripping the roof-guttering and steadying herself, she found she was about three metres away from where the man was sitting. The child looked very cold, but was far too young to realise his peril.

'Hello!' said Margaret, and, as the man turned to look at her, she managed to force herself to smile at him.

That was the prelude of a conversation. It went on for an hour and a half, and gradually, so slowly, Margaret managed to get the unhappy man to tell her his story and why he no longer felt he could go on living.

As the policewoman talked and talked to him, and listened with total concentration to what he said so that he would feel more confident, she inched her way slowly along the rooftop gully towards the parapet. She moved with such caution that the man did not take in the fact that she was gradually getting nearer to him and his baby son.

She began to make some progress. She felt that she had started to persuade him that even if he himself felt he must end it all, he should not take his child with him. She talked calmly, as if there was no hint of a crisis, though it was not easy to be calm with the raw wind cutting through her uniform. She could feel her hands shaking.

Slowly, or so it seemed to her, the look of determination in the man's eyes was starting to weaken. Meanwhile, though she did not dare take her eyes off him, Margaret was able to hear tiny sounds that told her policemen had

taken up positions on the roof not far from where the battle of words and feelings was taking place.

At last came the moment towards which she had been working. She was now only a metre away from the father and son. The time had come for action.

She leapt forward in the narrow gully, forced one of her arms round the baby, and gripped the father's coat so firmly with her other hand that by toppling backwards, she was able to pull him off his balance and towards her.

There was a short, tense struggle and the man released his hold on the child. From behind Margaret a policeman reached out to steady her, then, grabbing the man by his shoulder, he managed to pin him against the roof so that he could neither break loose nor jump.

With infinite care, Margaret turned round and handed the baby to safety. Meanwhile, the policeman, who was still holding the man firmly, called to his colleagues for help. Happily, no help was now needed. The man was no longer capable of putting up any sort of a struggle and allowed himself to be led off the roof and down into the house.

Only now did Margaret look down to the street once more, because far below her there was a sound of cheering. People were cheering her!

Then she glanced back at the narrow gully along which she had so perilously climbed. Just for a moment she closed her eyes.

For she realised now how very close she had been to disaster at that moment when she had jumped forward to grab the child from his father's arms. If the man had struggled just that little bit harder . . .

She suddenly felt sick and found herself shaking from head to foot.

She heard a voice saying: 'Come on!' and it seemed to be coming from a long way away. Helpful hands were stretched out towards her and she was given a hot drink. She was deeply grateful for that and grateful that when she had been congratulated and cheered, she was told: 'Go home. Don't come back on duty today.'

She found she was a heroine. She was on television. Her picture was in the morning papers, showing that dramatic leap of hers. Many people sent her flowers and presents and some total strangers even proposed to her. Then some time later she got her greatest reward. For her bravery and her ability to cope with the grim situation, a situation above and beyond the call of ordinary duty, Margaret Cleland was awarded the George Medal.

11   *The Highwayman was a Girl*

There were not many people about to spot the lone rider galloping south towards the English border that July day in 1685. It was just as well. In the wild country where Scotland and England met, a horseman on his own could never feel completely safe, and this particular traveller was not a man but an eighteen-year-old girl.

Grizel Cochrane slowed her horse down. He was the most powerful mount that she had been able to find in Edinburgh, but she had to rest him as much as possible. Her beloved father's life depended on nothing going wrong with her plan, and he was lying in the grim Tolbooth Prison in Scotland's capital under sentence of death. He would be beheaded if he was lucky. If he was unlucky, he would suffer the appalling fate of being hanged, drawn and quartered.

She anxiously scanned the narrow road ahead of her and the lonely hills around her for any sign of life, but there was nothing to be seen. It was time to be moving on once more.

Grizel's father was Sir John Cochrane, who had been thrown into prison for taking part in an unsuccessful rebellion against King James II of England and VII of Scotland.

James had a positive genius for upsetting his subjects!

After the rebellion had failed, Sir John had been betrayed to the King's soldiers by one of his own family, and had been imprisoned as a traitor after being marched through the streets of Edinburgh bareheaded and bound. Another person on that march was the Public Executioner ...

Grizel had visited her father in the Tolbooth as often as she was allowed to. On her last visit she had heard that his death warrant had been personally signed by King James and was now actually on its way from London to Edinburgh, carried by an official mailman. The journey usually took eight days along a regular route, and as soon as the warrant arrived, Sir John would be executed. It was as simple and final as that.

'If only we had a wee bit more time, lassie,' said her father to her hopelessly. 'I've petitioned the King for mercy, but if yon warrant's already on its way, I'll no' have a head on my shoulders by the time the petition reaches him.'

He explained to the anxious Grizel that the death warrant was due to reach Berwick-on-Tweed in Northumberland in a few days' time, and it would be in Edinburgh just two days later.

For a moment Grizel could think of nothing but her father's impending doom, then suddenly her heart missed a beat. She had thought of a way of stopping the mail.

'I must away now, Father,' she said, kissing him fondly, 'but never fear. Something will happen, I'm sure.'

The next morning she rode out of Edinburgh, as the sun was beginning to rise. In a bundle tied to her saddle was a man's cloak and a pair of pistols. She was dressed as a servant girl. If anyone should stop her she was going to tell them that she was delivering the horse she was riding to her mistress.

After two days of hard riding and resting, Grizel reached the border town of Berwick-on-Tweed on the English side of the border. She went straight to the house of her old nurse, some six kilometres beyond the walls of the town, and when the old lady had finally recovered from the shock of seeing her so unexpectedly, she outlined her plan to her.

'See, here are two pistols and a horseman's cloak,' said Grizel, undoing the bundle she was holding. 'Now, where are the clothes that my foster-brother used to wear when he was a wee bit younger? Have you kept them? I do so hope you have! He was but a skinny lad when I knew him. Surely his breeches will fit me?'

They did!

Grizel's plan was either to steal the death warrant from the mailman in open country by pretending to be a highwayman, or to steal it from him when he was at Belford, some way south of Berwick. He was due there at six o'clock that very morning.

Dressed as a youth, she rode the thirty or so kilometres to Belford and found that the mailman had arrived on time and was snatching a few hours' sleep in the inn that served as an official stopping place for the letter carriers.

Grizel asked the landlady to draw her some water from the well, which was some way from the inn, then she crept stealthily into the room where the mailman was sleeping – mercifully – very soundly.

He was using his mail bags as a pillow! There was no hope at all of getting hold of them without waking him, but at least she could get at his pistols, which were beside him on the rough bed.

Slowly and very carefully she lifted the pistols and, one at a time, emptied their charges. Then she quietly slipped from the room, had a much-needed meal, and was on her way north again before the mailman awoke.

She rode to a crossroads and waited.

After an hour or so she sighted the mailman cantering along towards her. When he drew level with her she called huskily: 'Hullo there! I'm Edinburgh bound. May I ride along with you, friend?'

'I'll be glad of your company, young lad,' said the mailman, a tough-looking individual in his twenties. 'It gets mighty lonesome in these 'ere parts, even if it don't get mighty dangerous – and it gets that sometimes, I can tell you!'

They rode together for some kilometres, talking in a friendly manner, until they reached a lonely stretch of road near a hamlet called Buckton. Then, after a quick look round to see that no one else was near, Grizel whipped out her pistols, swung round facing the mailman, and roared as fiercely as she could: 'Hand over your mailbags or you're a dead man!'

The unfortunate mailman, shaken by this sudden turn of events, went for his own guns and fired at Grizel's head.

Nothing happened! Furiously he flung his useless weapons to the ground and leapt out of his saddle. He rushed towards Grizel and bravely tried to grab her horse's reins, but she was too quick for him. She started to canter away with the mailman in hot pursuit.

After getting him some way from his horse, she suddenly swung round, galloped past him to where his horse was standing idly watching the proceedings, and seized its bridle.

Moments later, she was racing off with both horses as

the air resounded with the mailman's shouts and curses.

Grizel sped over to a clump of trees and, as soon as she was out of sight, pulled up and leapt to the ground. Eagerly, she grabbed the mail bags, cut them open and started going through their contents.

In the second bag she found a letter with a Royal Seal. With trembling fingers she opened it. It was her father's death warrant, signed by the King.

As soon as she had read it, she tore it up, putting the pieces in her bosom; then, finding some more death warrants, most of them of people she knew, she tore them up as well. She left the other letters in the bags as she had found them and rode back to her old nurse's home.

'I never thought I'd see you alive again, you bonny bold lassie,' said the nurse, hugging her.

'Och, I was lucky,' grinned Grizel. 'Now, into the fire with these!' and she got out the torn pieces of the death warrant and burnt them.

'You'll no be riding back to Edinburgh in those breeches, girl?' asked the nurse accusingly.

'No, I am not,' said Grizel firmly and changed back into her servant's clothes. Then she thanked her nurse and was soon on the road for Edinburgh once more.

As for the unfortunate mailman, history does not relate what he was doing at that moment, but there was no way of his getting the bad news back to London fast.

Meanwhile, Grizel rode back to Edinburgh in high spirits. She reached the house in the city where her mother was staying changed into her own clothes again, and went to the Tolbooth prison to see her father.

'Grizel, lassie, you may or may not have saved my life, but you've certainly made me very proud of you,' said Sir John when he heard what she had done. 'Now then, it'll take two weeks or so for the news of your naughty exploit to reach London. If my friends can reach the King's ear before he signs another warrant, we may yet get a pardon.

This is just what happened. Some of Sir John's good friends got to see King James and managed to persuade him that a huge fine was better than chopping off a head. The idea appealed to the King, who pardoned Sir John, but seized all his money and estates. Sir John got the estates at least back after James was chased off the throne in 1688.

As for Grizel, news of her feat did not leak out at once or she would have been punished, but when it did she became a national heroine. A stirring ballad was written about her, which became a popular favourite of the day. Everybody was thrilled by the exploit of 'Cochrane's bonny Grizzy'! And, like a good heroine should, she married and lived happily ever after. She became Lady Ross, but in Scotland she is best remembered as Grizel Cochrane.

12   Captive of the Sioux

'You need have no fear of Indian attacks,' the officers at Fort Laramie had told them. Considering the growing tension between Indians and whites in the West, it was not the wisest thing to tell the small band of emigrants heading for Idaho in July 1864, as events soon proved.

They had gone some 100 kilometres from the fort when suddenly a war party of some 250 Sioux appeared. At first they seemed friendly enough, but suddenly they attacked. Fanny Kelly, eighteen years old and only married nine months, saw her friends killed around her, but at least her husband might have escaped. He had been away from the wagon train cutting wood when the Indians attacked. Meanwhile Fanny, her five-year-old adopted daughter Mary, and Sarah Latimer and her eight-year old son, were marched to a spot where they were ordered to sit quietly – or else. In a nightmare trance they watched the havoc and the killings until at last it was all over.

Fanny was determined to survive if she could, but she was not a girl to sit quietly and meekly. Her friend Sarah was a photographer and had expensive equipment with her with which to take pictures of the miners in Idaho. When she saw the Indians smashing it to bits, she howled in

E

anguish until a Sioux raised his knife to end the noise for ever.

Fanny sprang up and without a thought of the consequences, rushed over to try and stop the killing. Instead of triggering off two deaths, not one, the very reverse happened. The Indian turned round to gaze admiringly at her, then he took off his splendid feather headdress and handed it to her.

Fanny did not at first realise that the gift meant she was safe and under his protection. She later learned that he was called Ottowa. She described him as 'very old, over seventy-five, partially blind, and very ferocious and savage looking.'

Night fell, and the captives began their march to the Indians' camp. Fanny managed to tear up small pieces of paper which she dropped along the trail, then she told her daughter to slip down from the horse they were riding and follow the paper. 'I'll follow later, darling,' she told the little girl, giving her a kiss.

It was a fatal error, for unbeknown to her mother, Mary was soon caught and killed. As for Fanny, the Indians beat her and threatened to kill her, no doubt sparing her because of Ottowa.

She really does seem to have been rather thoughtless, considering how brave and cool-headed she was, for she now proceeded to throw away a peace pipe Ottowa had given her. True, she had accidentally broken it, but it was a sacred object. The enraged Ottowa decided to kill her. She was to be tied to an unbroken horse, which would be whipped, and when it started to gallop, the Indians would loose off as many arrows as they could at her.

Fanny as usual had a bright idea and took out her purse. Many of the Indians knew something of white money,

having traded at forts, and welcomed the 120 dollars she distributed amongst them. Once she had explained just how much they were worth, all talk of killing ceased.

Fortunately, she had learned her lesson and did her best to behave. She was on her own now, for Sarah and her son had vanished, where to she did not know. In fact, they had escaped.

Soon she was in trouble again, for she was given a pair of stockings by a brave only to find that she had provoked a feud. Ottowa's brother-in-law was the donor of the gift and promptly had one of his horses shot by the chief. So enraged was he that he raised his bow and aimed an arrow at poor Fanny, who started saying her prayers.

She was in luck once again, for a young Indian called Jumping Bear rushed at the archer and grabbed the arrow before it could be fired at her. The various parties paused and calmed down, Ottowa giving his brother-in-law another horse to soothe his feelings.

They reached the Sioux village, where Fanny found herself installed in Ottowa's tipi along with the old man's six wives. She was not expected to be a seventh, and she got on well with most of the wives. However, wife number one was a bad-tempered old woman. Another Indian woman asked Fanny over for a meal and Ottowa decided to go too. His senior wife was so furious that she went for Fanny with a knife. Fanny started to run and Ottowa tried to calm his wife, only to be stabbed several times himself.

At this, the wife's brother, deciding that the white captive was the cause of all the trouble, took his gun out and fired several shots at her, missing Fanny but hitting Ottowa. Things calmed down after that and Fanny found herself nursing her protector's broken arm, Ottowa being convinced that she was 'strong medicine'. History does not relate what happened to Ottowa's number one wife. In her book, *My Captivity among the Sioux Indians*, Fanny simply wrote: 'I never saw the wife of the chief again.'

By now she had learned that good behaviour was best, and so successful was she, so hard did she work, and so cheerful was she at all times, that the Sioux men began to admire her enormously. They compared their own women unfavourably with her and christened her 'Real Woman'.

So it was hardly surprising that when the Army found out where she was and began to negotiate for her release, the Sioux were not in the least keen to let their prize go. Men came to the camp to try and get her away for reward money, but she was suspicious of them. Meanwhile she saw the grim results of fights with the whites and her determination to keep cheerful must often have flagged.

Finally, she found herself transferred to another tribe of the Sioux nation, who were eager to exchange her for a reward. She thought this was a ruse to allow the Indians to get into Fort Sully and capture it. However, help came unexpectedly. The Indian who had grabbed the arrow destined for her heart now came to visit her. It was Jumping Bear and he proposed to her!

Fanny genuinely liked him, but had no intention of settling down as a Sioux. She said that he must prove his friendship by taking a message to the fort, warning its occupants that they were likely to be attacked. She did not tell him what was in the letter, except that it contained good things about him (which it did). Historians think that Fanny was wrong about the threatened attack, but she thought she was right at the time, which is what concerns us.

The Indians now took Fanny to the fort with a huge escort of mounted braves. The garrison, fully alerted, took no chances. A few chiefs were allowed in, the soldiers handed over the agreed reward – three horses and a large supply of food – and that was that. After more than five months Fanny was free.

It was some weeks before the greatest moment of all came. A soldier rushed up to her and said: 'Mrs Kelly, I have news for you. Your husband is here!'

'Language fails to describe our meeting,' Fanny was to write, noting how he had aged in just a few months and his hair was flecked with grey. He broke the tragic news to her of little Mary's death, though she had feared as much long ago. Now was the time to begin life again. Sadly, their happiness did not last long, for in 1868 he died of cholera. Three years later her famous book came out. Apart from its thrills and its terrors and tragedy, there is one fact that shines through it. Despite everything, she half enjoyed being an Indian!

13   Nightmare Journey

The storm was lashing the sea into a frenzy as the girl began her perilous climb up to the light at the top of the ladder. If she failed the lives of scores of sailors in gale-wracked ships would be in danger. Gritting her teeth as the howling tempest seemed to be trying to tear her from the tower, fifteen-year-old Ethel Langton inched her way upwards.

Ethel lived with her parents – they called her Deno – on an old disused fort off the small town of St Helens, near Bembridge on the Isle of Wight. Their unusual fortress home was a kilometre off shore and had been used as a searchlight station in the First World War, which had ended in 1918. Now, eight years later, it main purpose was to house a vital navigation light to help ships approaching Portsmouth and Southampton, and to make sure that they kept off the dangerous Bembridge Ledge and its treacher-ous sandbanks.

In good weather you could – and you can – get from the mainland to the fort with no more than wet legs. In a bad storm, however, even a modern lifeboat is hard put to it to make the crossing.

The lamp that Deno was aiming for was on top of a

platform about twenty-five metres above the sea. To get at it involved climbing up a steep ladder. Deno's father's job was to fill the reservoir of the oil-burning light, trim and light the wick, and wind the mechanism each day. But that tempestuous night in March 1926 found him and Deno's mother trapped on the mainland.

It was a Saturday, and the pair had rowed across to do some weekend shopping in Bembridge, leaving their daughter and her Pomeranian dog, Badger, in charge of the fort. Deno was used to being left on her own. Then the storm, one of the most savage for years, suddenly erupted. The Langtons were cut off from home.

At first Deno had not been in the least worried. She was used to storms and felt sure even this near-hurricane would soon blow itself out. But instead it got steadily worse.

So did the food situation. Deno and Badger soon finished what little bread there was and later made do with a loaf she made with some flour she found in the pantry.

'I must keep the light going,' she kept telling herself. 'I mustn't let it go out for a single moment,' and when darkness fell, she went out into the teeth of the gale.

At first the walls of the fort gave her a little shelter, but not for long. When she was only a few steps up the seven metre ladder that led up to the platform with the lamp on it, the full shattering fury of the gale hit her.

Her foot suddenly slipped, and for an awful moment she hung on by her hands alone, as the wind slammed her hard against the ladder. Then it seemed to change its mind and try and wrench her away from it altogether.

Finally, drenched, blinded by the spray, and deafened by the roar of the wind, she managed to reach the top. She did not dare stand up, but crawled slowly towards the lantern hatch. Once inside, she lit the lamp, crawled out

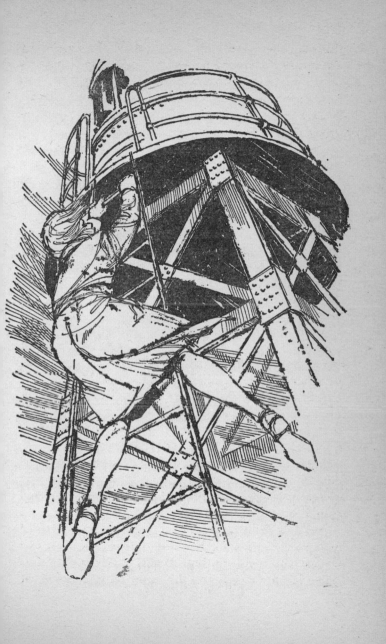

again, and began climbing down the ladder, which was just as grim an experience as climbing up had been.

Watchers on the shore were astounded when the light went on, and they were to go on being astounded, for Deno was to keep the light burning for three long nights. She did not sit back and hope for the best: she climbed up at regular intervals. In between her daring trips, she dozed, played with Badger, read, and played patience.

By the Tuesday morning there was no oil left, to the consternation of Deno. But help was near. Three fishermen were on their way in a motor boat, risking the dangerous crossing because of the fear that Deno might be starving. They at last reached the fort and one of them, George Smith, struggled through the surf carrying food.

He found Deno asleep, but Badger started barking and she awoke to see her rescuer. 'How are mother and father?' was the first question she asked.

Later that day, Mr and Mrs Langton arrived, carried across the still-rough water in a lifeboat. There was a wonderful reunion between Deno and her proud parents, to say nothing of the excitement of Badger.

'I was not a bit frightened,' Deno told a local reporter the next day, 'but I did become very anxious when the oil ran out.'

Her bravery hit more than the local headlines, and many people felt that she should get some award. In fact, she got several. She was awarded the Lloyd's Bronze Medal for Meritorious Service, a special award of a Canadian five-dollar piece surrounded by maple leaves from the St George's Society of Canada, and the Lifesaving Guards' medal.

As for her parents, first of all they gave her her birthday presents – that terrible Saturday had been her birthday! –

and then they had a silver clock inscribed with her nickname Deno and gave it her to commemorate her marvellous feat. 'I am very proud of my daughter!' Mr Langton told the press. And Deno's grandchildren are still proud of her now.

14   *Where has Mollie Got To?*

It happened one night in the town of Kohat, now part of Pakistan but once a key post on the frontier of British India. Fierce Afridi tribesmen with a grudge against the British broke into a bungalow belonging to a Major Ellis. The major was away, which made it easier for the intruders to kill his wife and seize his seventeen-year-old daughter Mollie.

Mollie was a slightly built girl not long out of school. The killers rushed her out of the bungalow in her nightdress. She had nothing on her feet, but they made her run across fields and into the surrounding hills, where they laid low for a day.

Mollie rested, shaded by a rock and still stunned by what had happened, while her kidnappers used binoculars to watch the troops who were hunting them. Then that night they started out again. Someone gave her his coat, while another ferocious-looking tribesman found her some leather-soled socks which gave her torn feet some protection.

The going got rougher and rougher as they cut deep into the Tirah, a vast area beyond British rule. As they climbed towards the mountains it grew colder and colder, but at last they reached their destination. Mollie knew the facts of life on the North-West Frontier, knew she was lucky to be alive in the house to which she had been taken, and also knew that she might die at any minute. Bravely, she waited for the rescuers she knew might never come.

The kidnapping occurred in 1923 and caused a sensation, not least because no one could understand why it had happened. In charge of the investigation was Sir John Maffey, Chief Commissioner of the North-West Frontier area. He was stationed in its capital, Peshawar. Into the local bazaars, always hotbeds of gossip and rumour, went his men to try and find out just why Mollie had been taken, and, finally, the truth was discovered.

The killers had earlier murdered a colonel and his wife, but there had not been enough evidence to convict them. Later, they were in trouble again and a police raid was carried out. Some of the gang escaped in women's clothes, but they were rounded up despite their disguises. As they were marched away, their wives howled derisively at them for dressing as women.

Two of the Afridis, the gang's leaders, Ajab Khan and his brother Shahzada, avoided arrest. They swore to avenge the humiliated men – and kidnapped poor Mollie. They were now demanding a free pardon for the whole gang. If not, Mollie would die.

It was useless sending troops after her, or police, because where she was being held was outside British rule, and anyone trying to rescue her would probably be killed. So would Mollie.

Sir John had a brainwave. There was a nursing sister at the local hospital, a Mrs Lilian Starr, whose husband had been murdered before her very eyes some years earlier by wild Afridis. Despite that, this saintly woman went on working and tending sick tribesmen so well that they came from as far away as Afghanistan to be nursed by her. She had travelled widely, and there was hardly a village in all that dangerous country that did not have at least one person whose life she had saved.

'Mrs Starr,' said Sir John. 'Will you go across the border and try to find Mollie Ellis, then stay with her until you are both rescued?'

'Of course!' said the brave woman, knowing that she could be going to her death.

The pair set out by car the next day to a point where Sir John's Indian assistant, Khan Bahadur, was waiting for them with a band of forty tribesmen. The Khan was an Afridi and clearly just the man for the job, but Mrs Starr was a little startled by some of the tribesmen with him. She later described them as a 'motley crew with rough black beards, dark, slate-grey clothing, their belts packed with cartridges, each with a rifle slung over his shoulder as though it was nothing more than a match in weight.'

They were friendly enough, though, and one of the party turned out to be a Mullah, a religious leader named Abdul Haq, who would help smooth their path.

Saying farewell to Sir John, Mrs Starr and her escort plunged into wild country where most people had never seen a white woman. Naturally, the women in the villages were amazed and thrilled to see her. The men, too, were impressed. 'Ha!' said one after a conference in which she had taken an active part, 'the woman understands. Now we know why the British rule Hindustan. Their women are as their men!'

At last they reached a village with real news for them. 'The girl is still alive and well,' said a man, pointing to the mountains. It was vague enough, but it gave them a glimmer of hope.

They were heading hopefully for the Khanki Bazaar, where the gang were known to live, though, of course, there was no reason to suppose that Mollie was necessarily being kept there. The Bazaar turned out to be a number of forts at the end of a valley, with houses scattered round about them. When they got there a message awaited the Mullah. It was from another Mullah and read:

> It is very necessary that you should not come in with the Englishman; if so, then this no pardon. Absolutely, lady-doctor and her company are prohibited. This is very urgent order. In default of this there will occur very long fighting.

What on earth did it mean? They had no Englishman with them. The mystery was solved though. The Mullah believed that one of the escort was an Englishman in disguise.

Though this mistaken belief was sorted out, the situation became more and more complicated. It would take a whole book to describe the tortuous events, discussions, arguments, threats and misunderstandings of the next three days during which Mollie's life hung by a thread, but basically the facts were simple enough. Her kidnappers were always liable to rush her to Afghanistan, where it would be virtually impossible to recover her – assuming that she could stand the journey there. And the kidnappers were making impossible terms for her release: a colossal sum of money plus an amnesty for every member of the gang and for the murderers of the colonel and his wife. These were turned down by one of the Khan's men, who referred to a proverb about a frog who wanted to be a bull! Finally, Mrs Starr was brought to where Mollie lay on a bed, tired but unharmed. It was a wonderful moment for both of them.

Suddenly, heavily armed men burst into the room. Two of them were the brothers who had kidnapped her, the others members of the gang. Shahzada angrily started shouting at Mrs Starr.

'You must write a letter now,' he erupted, waving his rifle. 'An army is on its way here and will burn our houses.'

'I know nothing of armies,' said Mrs Starr, refusing to be intimidated.

Another man rushed in. 'It is too late,' shouted Shahzada again. 'They are burning our houses and killing our women.'

In fact, nothing so dramatic was happening. It was just another fight between various factions in the whole, by now mad, affair. It was also the last gamble of the murderers. The local Mullah had little time by now for the murderers. He started cursing them so vividly that the wretches went down on their knees, took off their turbans, and laid them at his feet.

'Forgive us! Forgive us!' they cried. 'Take away the curse.'

'I take it away,' said the Mullah. 'Now, take these creatures out of my sight.'

The humbled gang were now unable to get anything but the mildest concessions from the British. They agreed to exchange Mollie for two small-time thieves who were languishing in Kohat jail and who were not involved in the killings.

Mollie and Mrs Starr still had to wait until the two thieves were released, so while the former regained her strength, the remarkable Mrs Starr began treating tribes-

men and their wives. She could hardly cope with the rush, and she remains a legend in that wild area to this day.

On the night of 22nd April the great news came through that the prisoners had been released. Mollie and Mrs Starr bade farewell to the Mullah and other friends they had made, and, with their escort, rode away on horses. It was just three days since Mrs Starr had first met Mollie, but it seemed a lifetime. Half way home they met the two prisoners, who could hardly believe their luck.

They reached British territory at night and came face to face with Sir John. It was not long before they rode into Shinawari fort, where a touching reunion took place between Mollie and her father. He was told how brave she had been and was very proud of her. Now it was time to go home, to a home without a wife and a mother.

Mollie said goodbye to her wonderful rescuer and to those who had accompanied her, while Mrs Starr got used to being acclaimed as a heroine in Britain and India alike. She put a stop to stories that she had ridden into danger armed to the teeth and leading a bunch of ferocious tribesmen! Killing was not her business.

Medicine and healing were, however, and soon she was back in her beloved mission hospital. As for Mollie, she retired from the stage of history, but there was one last act to be played out in Tirah. Her mother's murderers were banished for ever by their own people.

15   *The Spanish Girl*

If the capture of the town had been a blood-drenched nightmare, what happened next was like a scene from hell. Yet of it came one of the great love stories of history between a dashing young British officer and a fourteen-year-old Spanish girl.

It was 1812 and the Peninsular War in Spain was at its height. The British under their general Wellington, soon to be a Duke, were freeing Spain from the French with Portuguese and Spanish help. Not all Spaniards wanted to be free. The strongly fortified town of Badajoz was full of pro-French citizens. It was taken at terrible cost, thousands of British and Allied troops being killed in the assault.

In those days, if a city did not surrender after a major breach had been made in its walls, the attackers considered that they had the right to pillage it after it fell and extract their revenge. The British took full advantage of this; in fact they behaved like drunken madmen. Their officers lost all control as the men roamed the streets inflamed by drink, plundering and killing. Wellington's magnificent army had gone to pieces. Finally, he managed to restore order by erecting a gallows in the main square with armed Portuguese troops beside it.

Before this, when the horror was at its height, two Spanish girls had been trapped in their house, clutching each other in terror, as the troops approached. Flames rent the sky, musket shots rang out, and they could hear the soldiers' drunken yells getting nearer every minute.

The younger girl was Juana Maria de Leon, who was just out of a convent school and had come to stay with her sister, whose husband was away at the wars. Soon the soldiers were battering at her door.

It did not give way, so they shot the lock off and rushed in.

They wrecked the house and stole its contents, but the two girls managed to escape the drunken men, even though their necklaces were ripped off and their earrings were torn off, leaving their ears bleeding.

Through the terrible streets they ran, hiding when necessary.

'We have only one hope,' said the elder sister. 'We must throw ourselves on the mercy of a British officer. There must be many outside the walls.'

There were some inside them, trying to protect women and children. Some died at the hands of their own men. Meanwhile, the girls ran on and at last came to the main British camp.

Outside a tent stood two young officers of the Rifle Brigade, Harry Smith and Johnny Kincaid. They were discussing the battle in which so many of their friends had died. Suddenly, two women in black appeared before them. Their mantillas covered almost all their faces and they looked and moved like princesses. The older girl threw back her mantilla and told their story. When it was over, Juana, too, threw back her mantilla and both young men promptly fell in love with her!

Harry had a slight advantage in that he had served in South America and knew some Spanish. 'She had the figure of an angel, with an eye of light and expression which inspired me with maddening love which has never abated under many and most trying circumstances,' he later wrote.

Juana was swept off her feet too. They fell violently in love and a fortnight later were married.

Her sister warned her to be careful. 'He is only the younger son of a doctor,' she said. 'You are the daughter of a nobleman.'

'What is that to me!' said Juana. 'I love him.' Even the fact he was Protestant and she Catholic made no difference, nor that a war was raging all around them.

There was no question of her staying behind. She would follow her Harry, who was ten years older than her, everywhere. That was the way both wanted it.

Wellington gave his permission, having a soft spot for Harry, who was a born soldier; indeed the great man agreed to give the bride away. There was no time for a honeymoon for Captain Smith and his child bride. Like a number of other officers' wives, she followed the flag.

Harry gave her a fine horse and taught her to ride. His trusty servant West was assigned to guard her and a woman was hired to act as maid. Many nights they slept in the open, sometimes on a battlefield. Juana loved every moment of her new life and Harry's men adored her. It was a tough life and they loved the way she shared all their hardships. As we have seen, they were a rough lot, but not when she was around. They adored her even more when she broke a bone in her foot after falling from her horse, but refused to be left behind. It was weeks before it could be attended to properly, but she never left her place in the baggage train on the march, and was with Harry at the end of each day's march.

So day after day went by to the sound of trumpets and drums and cannon fire. On the night after the battle of Salamanca Juana slept on the battlefield on fresh-cut wheat, her hand holding her beloved new horse. In the morning she found that he had eaten her bed from under her.

Several times she thought that her Harry had been killed and searched the battlefield for him, but he bore a charmed life. As well as her horse Tiny, she now had a dog, a pug named Vitoria after one of Wellington's victories. Her family was complete!

At last the war ended, but the lovers were parted for a time, Harry being sent to America to fight in a war with the United States. Months later, the lovers were reunited and found themselves hastening from Harry's home in England to Belgium. For Napoleon, defeated and exiled in 1814, had escaped, and Europe was in an uproar once again. Harry took part in the great and final battle at Waterloo in June 1815.

The slaughter was appalling. Juana heard that the battle had been won, but could not get word of Harry. She was in Antwerp with the wife of the city's commandant, Colonel Crauford, and, to the alarm of them both, announced: 'I will join my Harry whatever shape fate has reduced him to. With West and other servants bringing baggage and spare horses, she set out towards the battle-field.

She ran into a group of riflemen.

'Yes, we knew (*knew!*) Brigade-Major Smith, mam! He's been killed,' said one of the men.

Her heart broken, Juana galloped on. 'I will die on the body of the only thing I have on earth,' she said to herself,

'and which I have loved with a faithfulness which few can or ever did feel, and none ever exceeded!'

She rode past the dead and the dying, the debris of war. The battlefield itself, even to a veteran like Juana, beggared description and was made worse by looters who prowled everywhere like wolves. It was no place for a woman to be, but on she rode.

She came upon freshly-dug British graves and wept. 'O God, he has been buried,' she thought. 'I shall never again behold him.'

Then she thought she spotted him and galloped over to the corpse, but it was not Harry who lay there.

Suddenly she saw an officer she knew and spurred over to him.

'Where is he?' she asked. 'Where is my Enrique?' That was the name she usually called him.

'Why he's as well as he's ever been in his life,' said her friend. 'He's not even wounded.'

'Don't deceive me,' the frantic girl implored him. 'The soldiers told me he was dead.'

'On my honour, Mrs Smith, Harry is alive! He's very anxious about you though. It's Brigade-Major Charles Smyth who is dead.'

'Then God has heard my prayer!' sighed Juana. Soon they were in each others arms.

Harry stayed on in the army after the great victory and, with Juana by his side, served in many parts of the world: Canada, the West Indies, Africa and elsewhere – wherever her beloved 'Enrique' was sent she went too.

In India in the 1840s she found herself in action once again, this time against the Sikhs. She and some other officers' wives were riding on elephants and had advanced to the head of a column to try and avoid huge clouds of suffocating dust. Suddenly, cannon balls enlivened the proceedings, several landing in front of the big beasts and rolling between their legs. Most of the wives became panic-stricken, not being used to action, but Juana calmed them down as best she could and led them and their very conspicuous steeds to safety. The only casualty was an elephant which lost part of an ear and raced away faster than elephants usually move. A few days later the wives were gathered in a tent enjoying a cup of tea when soldiers rushed in and ejected them moments before a huge mine exploded and blew the tent to bits.

Soon her Enrique was Sir Harry Smith, not Sir Henry. Sir Harry was good enough for him, and his Juana was Lady Smith. They were a most popular couple and two towns in South Africa were named after them, Harrisburg and Ladysmith. Finally, in 1860 Sir Harry died. Their forty-eight year romance was over. Juana survived another twelve years and was buried beside him at Whittlesey in Cambridgeshire.

If this storybook romance had been fiction, they would have died within minutes of each other, as we know Harry had hoped. Years before he had written her a loving, teasing letter which makes a suitable ending to this story:

> When I was first troubled with you, you were a little wiry, violent, ill-tempered, always faithful, little devil, and kept your word to a degree which, at your age, and for your sex, was as remarkable as meritorious, but please Almighty God, I shall have this old woman with me, until we both dwindle to our mother earth, and when the awful time comes, grant we go together at the same moment.

16   *Mary was a Pirate*

Having been brought up as a boy, it was perhaps hardly surprising that Mary Read should get a taste for being one. For she had been born in 1692, when opportunities to become a career girl were strictly limited.

Her mother had lost an infant son, but Mary – suitably dressed in male attire – made a very fine replacement. Only for a few years, though. Sometime in her mid-teens, Mary decided to branch out and ran away to sea.

After a spell as a sailor, she switched to the army, becoming a cavalryman and seeing plenty of action. Yet though she lived like a young man and fought like one, a girl she still was, proving it by falling in love with a handsome young soldier from Flanders (now part of Belgium).

History – and Mary's early history is mostly legend – does not relate exactly how she went about explaining that she was a she and not a he, but the young man was very pleased and the happy pair were married. Once their comrades learned the truth, they entered into the spirit of the thing and every officer gave the bride a present.

On the whole it seemed best to leave the army, and the lovers set themselves up as the proprietors of an eating-house, where they did a roaring trade, not least among their ex-comrades.

That might have been the end of the story, but Mary's husband suddenly died. As peace had now come, the young widow found herself short of money, so decided to become a man again.

Despairing of getting promotion in the army, she sailed for the West Indies dressed as a man once more. It was a fateful decision.

English pirates attacked her ship, and the crew, finding an Englishman aboard, recruited Mary as a likely lad to served under the Jolly Roger.

Eventually she found herself serving as Mark Read about a ship commanded by 'Calico Jack' Rackam. Mark, as other pirates noted, was an expert with cutlass and pistol, which may have helped her preserve her secret, but there was someone else aboard who had a particular interest in the handsome young sailor.

This was Anne Bonny, who had run away to sea in her teens as a female pirate. She wore no male disguise, though. The story goes that when she went into action she would change from her woman's clothes into shirt and trousers and fight as a man – as Mary always did.

Anne fell for the smooth-faced Mark Read and made it clear to him that she had done so. To straighten things out, Mary revealed her true identity and, after her shock, Anne and she became fast friends.

Now it was Mary's turn to fall in love. Rackam and his crew of cut-throats captured a ship in which there was a navigator named Tom Dean. Needing a navigator himself, Rackam spared the youth and put him to work.

Mary liked the look of him and soon felt she must reveal her secret to him. The young navigator was first startled, then delighted, while Mary, being a much more respectable girl than Anne, was soon looking forward to being a wife once again.

Alas, Tom fell out with a pirate, a dangerous thing to do for he was a sailor, not a fighter. The pirate challenged him to a duel. Mary, fearing for her Tom's life, went into action herself. She quarrelled with the pirate and challenged him.

'You scurvy knave,' she roared. 'You'll fight me first before you fight Tom.'

'It'll be a pleasure, you mangy varmint!' leered the evil-looking pirate. 'I'll kill 'ee first, then 'im, the swab!'

The next time the pirate ship anchored offshore, the crew landed to see the fun. First Mary and the pirate took a shot at each other with pistols and missed, then they went to work with cutlasses. The man was no match for Mary and died on the sands.

Meanwhile, there were ships looking for Rackam and finally a sloop commanded by Captain Barnet tracked him down in a bay. Rackam and his men were in the middle of a giant drinking spree and none felt like fighting. They tried to escape, but it was too late. Barnet sailed alongside and soon his men were swarming aboard the pirate ship and making short work of the drunken crew. The survivors were forced below, but there were still two in action on deck, Anne Bonny and Mary Read, both in male dress and both using their swords and pistols with deadly effect.

Between bouts with the boarding party, they cursed the cowardly dogs skulking below. Mary was so furious with them that she fired at them. Finally, both girls were captured, neither of them having been wounded. With the rest of the crew they were taken to Jamaica, where they were charged with piracy.

Rackam and the worst of his crew were executed, but Mary got her Tom off, convincing the authorities that he was no more than an ordinary seaman who had been made a pirate against his will.

And Mary and Anne? Both of them pleaded that they were pregnant and both by the rules of the day were spared for that reason. Anne's admirer had been Rackam and on the day of his execution, she was allowed to pay him a final visit. She spoke to him frankly.

'I am sorry to see you here, Jack,' she said, 'but if you had fought like a man you need not have hanged like a dog.'

Anne served a year in prison then returned to her home in America where she is said to have lived quietly and respectably. Alas, poor Mary caught a fever in jail and died. She deserved a better fate.

More Beaver Books

We hope you have enjoyed this Beaver Book. Here are some of the other titles:

Fortune-Telling Fun A Beaver original. A guide to all the different ways of telling fortunes, using numbers, paper, dice, dominoes or phrenology (the bumps on your head!) as well as the more usual crystal ball, astrology, palmistry, cards or tea leaves. Written by Gyles Brandreth and illustrated by Lim Mei-Lan

Shiva's Pearls. When Ottalie Temple's father dies, he leaves her a string of pearls, hidden somewhere in her uncle's big old house in Yorkshire. But before Ottalie can find the pearls, she realises other people are looking for them too . . . An exciting novel set in Victorian times for readers of nine upwards, by Harriet Graham

The Beaver Horse and Pony Quiz Book A Beaver original. See how much you know about horses and ponies by trying out some of the hundreds of questions on feeding, grooming and stable management, breeds, colours and markings, riding, showing and jumping in this book. Written by Sandy Ransford and illustrated by Christine Bousfield

These and many other Beavers are available at your local bookshop or newsagent, or can be ordered direct from: Hamlyn Paperback Cash Sales, PO Box 11, Falmouth, Cornwall TR10 9EN. Send a cheque or postal order, made payable to The Hamlyn Publishing Group, for the price of the book plus postage at the following rates:
UK: 22p for the first book plus 10p a copy for each extra book ordered to a maximum of 92p;
BFPO and EIRE: 22p for the first book plus 10p a copy for the next 6 books and thereafter 4p a book;
OVERSEAS: 30p for the first book and 10p for each extra book.

New Beavers are published every month and if you would like the *Beaver Bulletin*, which gives a complete list of books and prices, including new titles, send a large stamped addressed envelope to:

Beaver Bulletin
The Hamlyn Group
Astronaut House
Feltham
Middlesex TW14 9AR

341194